What Do Google Keywords Tell Us About Our World ?

A Nerdy Girl's Take on the World

By

Jamila Crockett

DEDICATION

This book is dedicated to my friends and family for their untiring support of all of my wacky dreams.

To all the self-proclaimed "Do It Yourself-ers" who just do it and don't sit just sit there.

To the techie community for your inspiration and cutting edge and innovative creations.

Viva la Internet!

CONTENTS

ACKNOWLEDGMENTS

Thank you Marcus for your encouragement and support.

Grandma *Love You*

Mie, Tiff, Dee Dee, & Tamika *Hugz*

TO MY 5,000 + Facebook family, friends, and subscribers *Thank YOU* for your virtual *group hugz*, love, support, and well wishes ALWAYS.
Smooches

To everyone I know, thanks for being in my life. You have made this world more special for me because you are in it!

1

Introduction

I know that what I am writing about is pretty nerdy but I am one of those girls who loves analytics and all things technical. I think if I would have played my cards right in college I would have dropped out and started a tech business like Bill Gates and Steve Jobs.

My computer "career" or more like interest started in high school in 1989 when our high school curriculum either allowed us to take a typing class or computers. I opted for computers because it seemed like cutting edge technology and most of all it was fun. I took Pascal and Basic using Commodore computers at the Lawrence Hall of Science during the summer program.

This was during the time when everything was DOS yet there were some leads in the areas of graphics with Macintosh having some of the most impressive black and white graphics you could imagine! I remember install Aldus pagemaker on my Mac Classic and thinking, "Wow! that's amazing that the pictures of a tiger having so much detail."

How times have changed I could have never imagined that gaming and graphics would get so realistic looking.

Anyways, I digress.

The point is that I have always had a fascination with computers and internet technology. I am one of the ones that shout, "Keep the Internet Free!" And at one point and time before it was officially illegal, I wanted to be a hacker because I thought that it was amazing that people knew how to read code and learn how to get beyond other code. It was only an amazement for the intelligence behind it and nothing more.

Instead of stepping out on the "new frontier" at the time I chose to do something "smart". What is smart anyways? I guess it depends on who you ask.

I happily and gratefully graduated from college with a degree in Community and Regional Development and started a business consulting nonprofits. My heart was and still is very much for the community however my love for computer technology and internet based products has never died.

2

How I Started My Quasi-Techie Life

As with most entrepreneurs, I began to accumulate so many hats along the way. I became annoyed anytime I had to learn something technological because prior to the dot com bust, things were changing so fast!

It seemed like every 10 months Microsoft in particular was coming out with new products and I felt overwhelmed trying to keep up. It was all too consuming and I thought that I had made the best choice by going into a social science as a career.

I neglected the fact that technology impacts multiple industries. No one could fathom the impact that computers would have on the world today, so many years in the future.

Well, at least in my small world view, I had no idea. They always say that hindsight is 20/20.

Well, let me tell you, if I would have known then what I know now about the emergence of so many tech companies and the expansion of silicon chips and ideas and the mere evolution of all what's possible today, it would have knocked my socks off and I would have invested more energy learning about computer programming, technology, and internet based business.

So, as I began to do more for my consulting business like marketing materials, basic web design at the time I completely loathed it because there was always a learning curve involved. I always thought in theory it would be better to have someone else do the work for me because by the time I learned how to do everything I would have wasted the time.

Back then anyways it was harder to even design a website that looked half way decent on your own unless you understood html or java or whatever language necessary.

Many times I hit a wall. Now-a-days you just hop on Weebly and BAM! you gotta website

with almost little to no effort on your part.
What a breeze they make it!

(SHAMELESS PLUG: My affiliate link to learn
more about Weebly:
http://www.weebly.com/link/dXJ8lg)

LOL!!! I know that's bad to plug...why not? I
like

them. They've made my life easier and I
usually don't stand behind a company or a
product unless I really believe in it.

3

Google Keywords Tool Reveals the Truth

As I began building my website, I used the invaluable tool, the

Google Adwords Keyword External Tool (www.adwords.google.com/o/Targeting/Explorer).

This is the best tool ever! Or one of the best tools ever.

What's great about this tool is that you can search the most popular keywords in the world in your given language. By putting in a keyword like "entrepreneurship" you get about 2.2 million searches globally. The word "entrepreneur" yields 2.7 searches, slightly higher. The the word "business" yields a whopping 101 million searches.

Why is this important?

Well for a novice SEO "expert" (and I say novice because there is still so much to learn) and I still don't consider myself a "techie", this information is profound because if you are building a website and you want lots of people to see it, you have to choose words that people are most likely to search.

I was in the process of finding out what type of keywords I could include in the meta tags so that more people could find my new Nonprofit Start up Course (portal) and I remembered that the first time I did this, I did a search for nonprofit and all things related to nonprofit and I began to think...wait a minute I am only putting words that only one million or less people would search.

Now, in normal thinking, one would think that one million is a large number in the internet world it isn't. I got really distracted and began to search words like Google and got a whopping 755 million global searches and I thought, "WOW! What else is getting major search results like that?"

I tried to plug other words in there that I thought most of the world would be concerned about like hunger,poverty, Starbucks, and nonprofits having less than 10 million searches. The big shocker for me was the famous answer that every Miss America contestant uses as the greatest concern, "World peace" came in at a low of 368,000; far less than even a half of a million searches.

I must say that it does not mean that people don't care of these issues, it just means that people may not care about them as much as Facebook which reaches approximately 3.76 billion searches worldwide per month.

I think these numbers really highlight really what people are thinking about the most, want to know more about, or have a greater priority for. Most of us have already become a slave to Facebook at one time or another or have admitted being addicted to it for various reasons, going through Facebook withdrawls, or just stopping altogether!

Maybe an ideal business would be a 12 step program for healing from Facebook? At least you are guaranteed to get some hits on your website if you have that type of product.

4

Calculations, Deductions,

Blah, Blah, Blah

These search results are showing really what people truly care about and what they want to know more about. It led me to believe that how much we truly care about things.

Before I go into the details of what my findings were, I must say a few things:

1) This by no means is scientific. I do not profess to be a scholar in research and analysis.

    Although I do know how to do some research and analytical work through my business, I am not using anything but the Google Keyword Tool, my brain, and my personal experience of what people say they like and have passion behind and what it shows in the number of searches that are found throughout the world.

2) These searches are global monthly searches, specifically in the United States, in English and were done via laptops and desktops, which means these numbers exclude mobile phone searches.

3) These searches were all conducted on the same day so that you can get a fair assessment that nothing major happened in the world on a given day outside of April 23, 2012. The numbers as I understand it from Google are derived from an average of 12 months by Google search users only. This means that no other search engine's data has been calculated in these numbers.

4) I chose Google search data for two reasons:

   1. Its the top search engine in the world and

   2. I prefer Google and its tools because they integrate well with each other and support the total analytics, conversion, sales, and tracking experience.

5) In no way, am I being paid or compensated in anyway from Google. I wish I were especially with my failed attempt with using adwords. LOL! That is another book altogether and yet another thing to really learn properly. There are so many facets to adwords that I would like to learn.

6) I separated the data in 5 categories:

1. Extra High (I know, really scientific sounding) with over 500 million searches,

2. High with over 100 mill searches

3. Medium with over 20 million search results,

4. Low with over 10 million search results, and

5. Very Low with under 10 million searches.

It was amazing how similar topics were within range of each other.

5

Hot Topic Indicators

As stated before, this information is purely my deduction. I just think that there is such a correlation between what our interests are and the searches that we conduct on a daily basis.

I can't help but wonder if these number of searches are prioritized by the number of searches. In the minds of Americans, our searches are revealing.

If you happen to be a Google Trend nut like me, you already know that what's hot today may not be hot tomorrow and I think that's why Google does an average of 12 months. If you don't know about Google Trends, check it out (www.google.com/trends).

There you can find all types of hot topics that trend throughout the day and based on what is happening in the world, you can see whether lots of people are talking about it.

I used Google Trends in the past whenever I got stumped on what to write on my blog. I would just go to Google Trends and see what the flaming hot and spicy topics were and just write around that. People would definitely come to my blog because of it.

Great way to get traffic to your blog!

The searches on Google search are less about tabloid or the daily news occurance and that's why I thought the Keywords tool would be a great indicator to what people were searching when no one was looking.

6

What Are These Numbers Really Saying?

Public vs. Private Life

I think people lead double lives, sometimes even more, but for the sake of this booklet, I will just say two. People have their public lives and their private lives.

The public life might be a minister of a prominent church who leads the Sunday prayer or prays over you in the prayer line. When he goes home and his wife isn't watching, he is on the porn site and on Google searching sex.

You might say, "Oh Jamila! You are horrible!" And I say, "Nope, I'm not." This is the world we live in. People do what they want to do when the lights are low and no one is there to police them. This is why we have crime, violence, taboo, and everything else under the sun that people are curious about but never come out and say it.

I think this is one of the many good things about Google search and other search engines is that we get a clear perspective unbiased about a person's natural curiosity. Even if the event only takes place once in a lifetime like the Great Depression, people still have an interest in it. And a certain number of people have an interest in the Great Depression and will search it more or less than something else. So for examples sake, 1 million people monthly search the Great Depression.

Now, maybe so many people have searched it because in the news our current economy has been compared to the Great Depression and people need some type of comparison on the way that it used to be back then. Well if we look at the same category, the under 10 million search results section, faith comes in at 9.1 million searches.

So, to me this says that even though there is poverty (2.7 million) and our economy may be compared to the Great Depression (1 million searches), the American people are still very optimistic because they have faith.

All of the high ranking keyword ideas in the Medium category that are associated with faith are: God (55.6 million), church (37.2 million), Christian, Jesus, Islam, and hope.

Politics vs. Education

The other areas that were shocking for me were the areas of politics and education.With all of the government budget cuts on education, one would believe that the government does not care about educating our youth. I see rioting over racial tensions and job closures. However, I have never seen a parade or riot over the lack of funding for elementary school education.

The search results for education are 101 million. The interesting thing is that when I look at the breakdown of this search, I see that most of the high ranking educational searches have to do with college, it education, training, and other vocational and adult education.

Primary school, elementary school, department of education, and many others fall well below in the Very Low Category of under 10 million searches. Does this mean that people place a higher priority over higher education and not enough on lower level education? Does this mean that the tax payers don't care about the education of our future children?

It gives the impression that the taxpayers are really okay with what's going on. Just like prayer in school. Somehow, it is now illegal to pray in school and yet prayer has a number of 13.6 million search results, whereas atheism (1 million) and agnostic (450,000) search numbers are way lower. How did that happen if prayer is more popular with those two combined?

In the next category, Low (10- 20 million searches) we see an interesting dynamic. Lady Gaga comes in at 20 million searches other popular topics of 20 million or under searches are keywords: wife, husband, girlfriend, consulting, economy, Muhammad, Quran, celebrity, and entertainment.

I am beginning to wonder if the level of excitement for all of these topics correlate with the search results. The other question that would need research would be, do certain topics speak more clearly to certain populations and whether those populations have equal or proportionate access to computers and the internet.

Although most people have access to computers, not everyone has the internet or even uses Google search.

This is why I say this is not scientific research because every member of society does not have the same access nor do they use the tools in the same ways. These are not polls but merely some type of standard deviation that I could discuss further had I passed Calculus. LOL!!!

The point is that these results are interesting and they do tell us something. What they tell us is that whoever uses Google on a regular basis also has certain searching tendencies and interests.

I think it would be a fairer assessment to say that Google keyword searches are representative of the population that uses Google, has internet, and an interest in whatever topic.

The question that I can't answer, but comes to mind is whether there are interests outside of those of the Google user population that has yet to be captured because they are just not on the internet? I am sure of it. I think it's safe to say that because so many people actually use the internet, that maybe the search results we are seeing are actually a representation of the majority of people in the US.

These types of things can be debated all day long.

7

Ok, Now Who Is Stuck in the Middle?

In the next Category in the Medium search result level (20- 100 million), we have woman and family tied at 83 million. Guns (55.6 million), race (45.5 million), and being funny (45 million) are more important than learning about Jesus (24.9 million) or the Bible (20.4 million).

Also, your heart, therapy, help, being young, sleep, food, clothes, real estate, money, spirit, trust, party, dance, and chocolate all are in this category as well.

So, what can be deduced? Well, we can say that because food, clothing, your heart, money, and spirit are all basic needs for a good life and these items came in at the Medium search result level, then maybe we don't view taking care of ourselves very high on the scale.

Somehow Facebook is up there, the very things that we need to survive are not the most searched.

Interesting.

It is also interesting to note that "life" and "live" were among the High level search results with 151 million and 277 million, respectively.

So, could we say that we want to live and have life but we don't really want to find out how? Or maybe it's the reverse. Maybe we would rather just live life than do the things necessary to improve our lives.

Another thing I found intriguing was the search words: woman, women, man, and men.

Word	Search Results
Woman	83 million
Man	226 million
Women	101 million
Men	151 million

There is an obvious disparity in the search results. Even though "women" and "men" are close in numbers, "men" is slightly in the lead.

The case of "woman" vs. "man" the word "man" more than doubles the use of man. Could it be from a historic perspective that more of man's stories are told online? Could it be that some root words involve the word "man"? Who knows? Are women searching for "man"? This is where I really wish that Google could get involved and clarify this for us.

Why is there such a difference in the use of these words? I can not answer this.

8

Who Are the High and Mighty?

The High Category includes search results 101- 499 million. Among these most searched words includes as mentioned, life (151 million), live (277 million), man (226 million), women (101 million), and men (151 million).

The big ones that I stumbled upon were: world (338 million), home (338 million), house (277 million), love (185 million), like (101 million), travel (101 million), business (101 million), baby (124 million), and music (277 million).

America came in at 124 million searches per month. "Job" and "email" each received 226 million searches per month.

These numbers speak more to what is going on in our world today. People are losing their homes, many are going into business for themselves, but many more are seeking jobs and using email.

It's funny how heart scored so low, yet love is high on the radar. Can you have love without heart? There are probably many definitions of love. Or are people just afraid of talking about the heart?

Also what is really funny to me is how party and dance are lower on the search result list and yet music is high up there! LOL!!! I guess people who don't know how to dance or party like music too!

These words center around high activity for what is happening today. People are having babies, looking for jobs, and trying to find or keep their homes.

These numbers make sense to me out of all of the categories. Nothing more to say about this level.

9

Now... the Moment

We've All Been Waiting For!

The Extra High Category of searches makes sense, yet behooves me the most because of all of the "most important" items that are below it on the priority scale.

Really?! Facebook is more important than family? Really?! I've heard of mother's neglecting their children because they are consumed with who "liked" their status.

A sample of the Extra High level of searches include:

Word	Search Results
face	3.76 billion
book	3.76 billion
Facebook	3.76 billion
"what to do"	Almost 1 billion
"how to"	500 million
Sex	500 million
Google	755 million
Game	618 million

As you can see, this is very interesting. People are wanting to know what to do and how to do it. They want sex and games. Facebook is probably the reason for the inflated results surrounding "book" and "face".

These results are not really surprising within themselves. The surprise to me is how they surpass everything that one would consider meaningful to everyday life.

10

Conclusion

So, are these results of value or is this a bunch of malarkey? Well, I think there is something that can be said about the number of search results we are seeing in these areas.

It's interesting not necessarily because we know these areas are popular, but its interesting because of how much more popular they are than the things that everyday people claim are the fabric of our lives or our core values.

Has Facebook replaced our core values or are the Extra High Category items an extension of our core values?

Are our true core values different from what we think or want to believe our core values to be as a society? We say that we value religious tenants, family, hunger, world peace, money, and elementary school education. Yet, our activities online, curiosities, and things we fill our heads with have nothing to do with what we say in our public lives.

So my question to you is do you want to live life and make your public life core values true values in your private life as well.

I am guilty of these tendencies of searching Facebook and putting Google or my business interests above those of family, as well. We all are not immune to this activity.

This informal data collection has really shone a light on our activities as a nation and maybe we can have a deeper perspective on what really matters in the end.

Its up to us to change this. The questions become have we evolved to this behavior and are we too far gone to turn back?

Here is a revolutionary thought:

Maybe we have always been this way but because no one has been monitoring our individual behaviors and activities over the course of human existence. We never knew how much we were out of alignment as a society with what we think vs. what we do.

Google Keywords External Tool and search results has pulled back the carpet (so to speak) on our society and revealed the truth about our behaviors. What we say in public is not consistent with what we do in private.

We are all guilty.

PS. I know you're itching to check your Facebook status! GO AHEAD!!! LOL!!!

thanks for reading my nerdy girl experiment

~Jamila

ABOUT THE AUTHOR

Jamila Crockett, Principal Consultant of JS Crockett Consulting, hobbies as a SEO and overall internet enthusiast.

This California native graduated from UC Davis with a degree in Community and Regional Development, emphasis in Organizational Management; completed the Management Development for Entrepreneurs Executive Management Program at UCLA; and earned a Certificate of Completion from CSU, Sacramento's Project Management program.

She currently lives in Southern California, while indulging in plenty of beach sunshine and all things SEO.